ESSENTIALS

DIGITAL
PHOTOGRAPHY
FOR KIDS

igloo

igloo

Published in 2006
by Igloo Books Ltd
Cottage Farm,Sywell,NN6 0BJ.
www.igloo-books.com

10 9 8 7 6 5 4 3 2 1

ISBN: 1-84561-425-9

Project managed by Metro Media Ltd
Editorial and design management: Adam Phillips
Author: Duane Harewood
Cover design: Andy Huckle
Text and layout: Tom Lynton and Andy Huckle
Picture credits: Photos.com, istock.com, Canon, Fujifilm, Epson, Eastman Kodak Company, SanDisk Corporation, Microsoft Corporation, Adobe Systems Incorporated, Serif (Europe) Ltd, Nokia, Corel Corporation, Hewlett Packard, Siemens, Nikon

Printed in China.

DIGITAL PHOTOGRAPHY

Welcome to the incredible world of digital photography. In this book, you will discover how to make the very most of your digital camera – from the best tips for taking the perfect picture through to using computer editing software to make your great photography even better!

INTRODUCTION TO DIGITAL PHOTOGRAPHY

Digital cameras can look a bit scary and complicated to operate, with lenses that zoom in and out, lights that flash and noises that go bleep. But the truth is that they are actually incredibly easy to understand and use. With a little practice, you'll be amazed how quickly you can produce fantastic results. In this chapter, we look at how you can save time and money by using digital equipment instead of old-fashioned film. You will also find out what other digital devices are currently available and how the whole process works.

You can have a lot of fun taking photos with a digital camera. That's partly why digital photography has become so popular. In fact, it's so popular that, in 2005, 140 billion digital photos were taken all over the world. Digital cameras have not been around for very long: the first ones were launched in 1994. But like the MP3 and DVD players, digital cameras have managed to make a great impact on our lives.

An old camera that shows how far technology has come.

WHY GO DIGITAL?

MP3 players are digital too!

With conventional cameras you would have to get your film to laboratories to be processed and developed into prints. Then you'd have to wait anything from an hour to a month before you could see your results. With digital cameras there is no need to spend hard-earned pocket money on expensive film or processing fees.

Competition is tough between camera manufacturers, so they are continually making better and better cameras and improving their technology. There are lots of fantastic digital cameras to choose from. This means that not only are older models or second-hand cameras fairly cheap, but you can currently buy a very basic, brand-new digital camera for less than the price of a meal out!

10 DIGITAL FACTS

1 See your pictures immediately.

2 Using digital cameras is less expensive than using film cameras.

3 Digital cameras are always getting cheaper.

4 You can shoot video on most digital cameras.

5 You are able to delete bad shots there and then.

6 You can improve pictures after you've taken them.

7 You can print pictures yourself from your own home.

8 Digital photography lets you share your pictures via email.

9 Digital technology is advancing all the time.

10 You can go digital for the price of a magazine!

A few years ago it was unimaginable to take a picture without using any film. But, in a digital camera, an image sensor replaces the film.

This image sensor (often called a Charge-Coupled Device, or CCD) turns light into electricity. Unlike a roll of film, you can use the same image sensor to take millions of photos without having to change or replace it.

HOW DOES DIGITAL PHOTOGRAPHY WORK?

A digital camera is like a miniature computer and, as with the other computers that you use, your camera will analyse the data that you put into it.

It may just look like a simple pattern, but this is the CCD that captures all your digital images!

WHICH TYPE OF CAMERA IS RIGHT FOR YOU?

If you don't already have your own camera, choosing the right camera for your needs is important. Your choice will probably be restricted by the amount of money you have to spend. But there are other things to consider when selecting a camera. When you hold a camera, make sure that it feels comfortable, isn't too bulky and the controls aren't too fiddly. See page 12 for details about the differerent cameras available.

WHAT DO YOU WANT TO SHOOT?

What will you mainly take pictures of? Will you want to take shots of your family and friends? Perhaps you'd like to take photos at sporting events such as football or hockey matches? You may prefer taking nature and wildlife photos when you are away on your holidays. Or it could be a mixture of subjects. Some digital cameras are better for certain subjects than others.

What do you want to take pictures of? Sports? Wildlife? Parties? School friends? Or your family? Whatever you want to capture, there's a camera out there for you.

WHAT WILL YOU DO WITH YOUR PICTURES?

The other thing you need to think about is what you intend to do with your photos once you've taken them. Will you be printing your pictures, emailing them or even posting them on a website? If you already have access to a computer, make sure that the camera will be able to link up to it.

A home PC is perfect for viewing, changing and storing your digital pics.

SHOPPING FOR A CAMERA

There are many places to find the perfect digital camera. Here are a few pointers:

- **Visit specialist photographic shops as well as general electrical stores.**

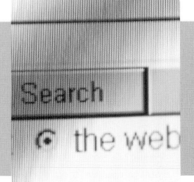

THE POWER OF PERSUASION

Perhaps you are lucky enough to already have access to a digital camera – one that's owned by your parents, brother or sister. If so, get as much practice with it as possible. This will help you decide on what features you want when you get your own camera. But if you do borrow someone else's camera, treat it with respect.

If you are trying to persuade your parents to buy a digital camera, it may be worth mentioning how much money they will save by not having to pay for film, processing and developing over the years. You could even offer to take some flattering photos of them – it's certainly worth a try!

- In addition to checking shops, keep an eye on internet sites for photo equipment bargains.

- Read photography magazines and surf online for the latest camera reviews.

- Ask to borrow your friend's or family's camera to see if you like using it.

DIFFERENT TYPES OF CAMERAS AVAILABLE

There is a wide variety of cameras available in the shops and online. At first glance they all appear to be very similar. The majority of digital cameras are compact and chrome coloured. Some have zoom lenses and most have an LCD (Liquid Crystal Display). They vary greatly in price, features and style, but you don't have to have a flash camera to get stunning shots. It's the images that you produce that are important, not the image of your camera.

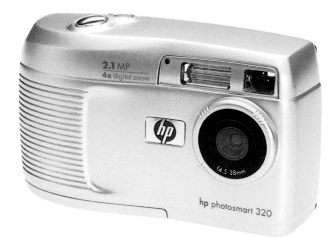

Good quality digital cameras needn't cost the earth.

Point-And-Shoot

In 2003 the first 'disposable' digital camera went on sale in the US. This was a basic 1.0 megapixel camera taking up to 25 pictures. The camera then had to be returned to the store to have the photos downloaded onto CD. However, reusable cameras are now so cheap that disposables aren't worth buying.

The 'point-and-shoot' camera is the simplest of all digital cameras to use. As the name suggests, you just aim it at your subject and click the shutter to capture the picture. Because these cameras are so easy to use, you can take photos very quickly without having to worry about operating any controls.

The only downside to these cameras is that they normally have a low number of megapixels. This will mean that the pictures may not be of good enough quality to print. If, however, you only want to view your pictures on a computer screen or email them to friends, this could be the best type of camera for you.

Semi-Automatic Compact

This type of camera will be more expensive and have more features than the point-and-shoot camera. Semi-automatic cameras can range between 3.0 and 6.0 megapixels, so they will also be capable of creating pictures that you can then play around with, print and enlarge.

The screens on the back of cameras help you organise your shots – like a mini PC!

Another good thing about semi-automatics is that they have zoom lenses, so you can get in closer to your subject. This is useful when you are not able to move in closer yourself – when you are at a sporting event, for example.

These cameras will also have a movie function so that you can shoot video footage. This type of camera should be able to cope with all of your needs and allow you to develop your skills.

SLR (Single Lens Reflex)

These cameras have a detachable lens and tend to be big, bulky and very expensive (£400 to £5000). They are used mainly by professional photographers and can produce very high-quality photos.

You'll probably have seen the paparazzi using SLR cameras with very long zoom lenses to take pictures of celebrities from great distances. Their shots can be seen every day in newspapers and magazines. Some of these cameras have over 16.0 megapixels.

SLRs are very, very expensive.

If you own one of these, you're probably a member of the press.

More Mobile Info

When selecting a new mobile camera phone, it's worth finding out how much your network will charge you (or the bill payer) to send and receive picture messages. Some companies will allow you unlimited picture messages or special deals if your phone is on a monthly contract. It is best to talk to whoever is paying the bill if you think an upgrade is in order!

It is also worth knowing that you can send a picture to a friend who has a non-camera mobile phone: they will receive a text message explaining how to view the image via the internet.

Unfortunately, mobile phones are very attractive to thieves so be careful where and when you use them. You can register your mobile phone so that, if it is stolen and recovered, it can then be returned to you. In the UK go to www.immobilise.com

Camera Phones

More and more mobile phones have cameras built into them. Most of them will have 1.0 or 2.0 megapixels and be able to record video and still shots. The picture quality will be low but that's fine if you just want to send pictures to other mobile phones. Camera phone technology is quite new and still being developed, so there won't be many features but they should have a flash and you can still get some quite decent results if you practise. Camera phones are great if you are constantly taking snaps and don't intend to print them.

OTHER GOOD WAYS OF GOING DIGITAL

Scanning

Did you know that there is a way of turning your old prints into digital photos even if you don't have a digital camera? You can do this by using a scanner.

A scanner looks like the top of a photocopier and works in a similar way. The scanner will have to be linked up to your PC or laptop; you may need to install some software in order for the computer and scanner to communicate with one another. Once the scanner has copied the photo, it can be saved on your computer. You'll then have the freedom to play around with or adjust the image on the screen.

Instead of just copying a photo with a scanner, you could actually use it to take a digital photograph. If you place an object onto the scanner it will 'take its picture' by copying the image and thus provide you with an original digital photograph. You are naturally a bit limited by what will safely fit onto a scanner, but you can nevertheless get some unusual and rather original pictures.

You don't always need a digital camera to take pictures.

Schools and libraries usually have an IT room where you can download and edit your digital photographs.

High Street

If you don't have access to a digital camera or a scanner, you can take your prints to a local high street photo lab and they will be able to put your pictures onto a CD so that you'll be able to view them and edit them on a computer. Although this method is very easy, it is not the cheapest option, so you should also check out your local public library. It could have an IT centre where members may be able to use scanners and computers without having to pay.

Multimedia

There are multimedia devices like MP3 players with cameras attached. Like phones, the main purpose of these is not to take pictures, so don't expect stunning results. But at least you can listen to some great tunes while you are snapping away.

PIXELS TO PICTURES

You may have heard the terms pixels and megapixels used a great deal in digital photography. When manufacturers advertise their cameras they will boast that their camera will give you lots of pixels for the price. It's therefore important that we discover what pixels are and how they affect our pictures.

Each photograph is made up of pixels, which stands for 'picture elements'. These are like tiny building blocks and when they are all connected together they form a whole picture. Each pixel holds a small piece of information or data about the picture: on their own they don't mean anything, but when they are all put together we can see the result.

The more pixels that a photograph contains, the more detail the final picture will have. However, the more pixels contained within the picture, the more room it will take up in the camera's memory.

Like building blocks, pixels don't mean much on their own, but put them together and all that changes.

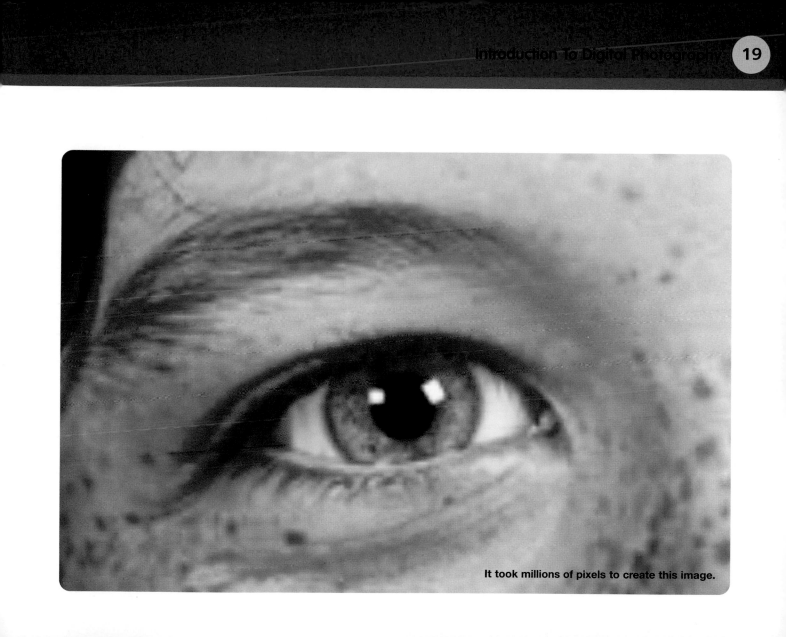

It took millions of pixels to create this image.

The three images here represent what happens when you use different amounts of megapixels – the one on the left shows a high resolution image. The one in the middle shows a medium resolution image. Finally, the one on the right shows a low resolution image.

GOING LARGE

Now we know what a pixel is, let's take a look at the megapixel. A megapixel is made up from one million pixels. So when you see a camera advertised with 1.0 megapixels, that's equivalent to 1,000,000 pixels. The most basic cameras have 1.0 megapixels.

Another important thing to bear in mind is that you should only pay attention to the number of 'effective

pixels'. This is the number of pixels used to record an image and this should be displayed on the box.

Although a camera may say it has a top range of 6.0 megapixels, you don't have to shoot at that number all the time: you will be able to take photos using fewer megapixels. For example, you could set your camera to 1.0, 2.0, 3.0 or 4.0 megapixels. This will be useful if you just want to email your photos, or are low on memory space or battery power. If you shoot using a low number of megapixels you'll be able to take more photos than you will when the camera's pixels are set high.

The number of pixels really matters when you intend to print and enlarge your photographs. Why not take a picture on a low megapixel setting and then take the same picture on a high setting? When you've done that, print the pictures and see the difference for yourself.

FILE FORMATS

Just like a computer storing any data, a digital camera has to put each picture into a file format. Some digital cameras will give you a choice of file formats in which to save your shots. To get good results it is important to know what you'll actually be doing with your pictures when you've got them.

JPEG

A digital camera will allow you to take photos and store them in different file formats. The most commonly used file format is the JPEG, which will appear as '.jpg'. JPEG (or Joint Photographic Experts Group, if you want to impress people) is the ideal format to use if you want to email photos or display them on the internet. Digital images contain a lot of information that you may not necessarily require, such as the date and time the picture was taken.

This system compresses the data that's contained within each image. By reducing the size to under 10% of its original size, the photo becomes much more manageable and this means that you will be able to store more photos in your memory. It also means that you'll be able to download them faster than you would larger files. Although a JPEG file is compressed, you won't lose too much quality in this format. Your camera may allow you to select a quality setting, so if you want the best quality then make sure you go for a high setting.

TIFF

Some sophisticated cameras will allow you to save a photo as a TIFF (Tag Image File Format), which is an excellent uncompressed file. It is used a lot by professional photographers who intend to edit and print their work. It gives the user a great deal of flexibility. However, a TIFF contains a lot of data and is therefore a large file, far from ideal if you intend using your photos on the internet.

There are various file formats – the one you choose will largely depend on what you intend to do with the pictures.

More File Formats

GIF: This stands for Graphic Interchange Format. It is another file that can be compressed and was designed especially to be used on the internet.

RAW: These files are made from uncompressed and unprocessed data. The name RAW refers to the state of the information.

Compress this picture and you'll lose quality, but it'll take up less memory.

COMPRESSING FILES

As mentioned before, there is a great deal of information included in each digital image. Understandably, there is information that contains the technical data needed to create the image, but there can also be less important information – for example, about the type of camera that was used.

A photographic file is much bigger than one that only contains words; many more details are needed to reproduce an image. Most of the time this is not a big problem, but sometimes – especially when you want to transfer or download images – large files can be inconvenient. No one wants to spend ages waiting to receive or send photos, so that's when compressing them becomes appealing. By compressing the file and reducing its size, such transfers can be done much faster.

However, there is a price to pay for compression and that is the possible loss of quality. When you are saving your photos as JPEGs your camera may give you the option of shooting with different levels of compression. If you use high compression you will be able to shoot more pictures of lower quality than on a low compression setting. If you are unsure what you would like to do with your photos until you've viewed them, go for low compression.

STORING THE IMAGE

After you have captured an image, the camera has to store it. With a conventional camera the image is 'stored' on the film. We know that digital cameras don't have any film, and although the image sensor can capture a picture it can't store it.

The most basic point-and-shoot cameras and currently most mobile camera phones have 'onboard' or 'internal memory' systems. This means that the memory is actually built into the body of the camera. It is a very straightforward system to operate. You just take as many photos as you can before the memory is full.

Then you will either have to start deleting photos if you want to keep shooting, or you'll have to go and

Memory cards come in all shapes and sizes.

download the images to free up some space on the camera. As you can imagine, if you are out and about taking pictures it is not always convenient to stop and download pictures. So that could be a problem for you if your camera has this kind of system installed.

Another option is to buy a camera with a removable memory device in the form of a memory stick or card. These commonly available devices come in various forms and prices. The great advantage of having this type of system is that you can remove the storage device when it's full and replace it with an empty one. This means that you won't have to interrupt your photo session halfway through.

Apart from giving you more freedom, a removable storage system will mean that you can upgrade your memory and therefore take more

If you want maximum storage, get a compact flash memory card.

photos before you run out of room. Memory devices are tough little objects and you'll be able to store millions of shots over the years.

VIEWING YOUR SHOTS

When you've taken your shots you can download them. Not everybody does though, especially if they take shots with their mobile phone. The majority of mobile phones are used as mobile photo albums before the photos are eventually deleted. However, after you've taken the picture the journey doesn't necessarily have to stop there.

You can link your camera up to a laptop or PC and view your shots on a monitor. This is a good idea because a bigger screen than the one on the back of a camera or the front of a mobile lets you see more detail in the picture itself.

Use a PC or laptop to view your pictures.

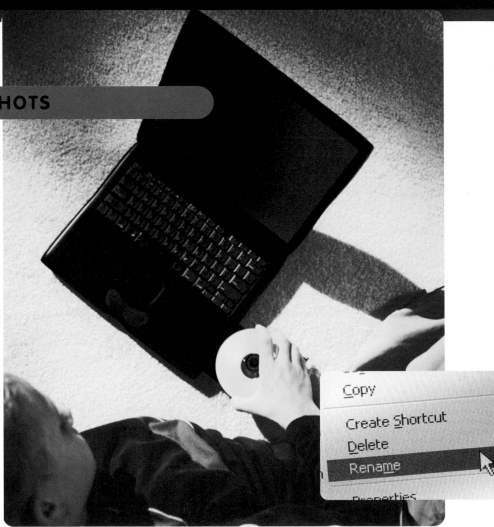

Once the photos are downloaded onto a computer's hard drive, you can transfer the images onto a DVD. Not only will that mean that you'll be able to view images via a TV screen, but you will also have a spare or backup copy of your photographs. A good tip when you have downloaded your images on a computer is to rename them. You'll see that each photograph will already have a code, but these codes will most likely be irrelevant to you. This will mean that if your photograph is labelled something like 33476.jpg, you can change it to something more descriptive, so that you can find it quickly.

Downloading your images also allows you to have fun altering your images using editing software.

Modern games consoles like the X-Box 360 will allow you to view your pictures on your home TV.

CHAPTER 2
GET GOING

In this chapter, we will take a look around a digital camera, from its very basic functions to some of the most advanced features. We'll also look at the different aspects and modes of the camera, explaining how you can use them to select the right settings at the right time. By the end of the chapter, you will have a complete understanding of how that small box of technology can help you create photographic magic. Let's get going!

A TOUR AROUND A DIGITAL COMPACT

 Shutter

When you press the shutter, you take the picture.

 Power input socket

If you can save your battery power, do it. Plug the camera into the mains via this socket.

 Microphone

Speak into here if you want to add a commentary to your film footage or leave yourself a message.

 Lens

This is how the camera looks out on the world, so make sure your fingers are not covering it when you press the shutter.

5 Power switch

The on/off switch. You won't get far if you don't switch your camera on!

6 Self-timer lamp

This will start to flash when you use the self-timer mode. It will start to flash faster just before the shutter is to be activated.

 Flash

This is where your burst of light comes from.

8 USB socket

This is a very useful socket: it allows you to link your camera to a PC, laptop, games console or printer.

1
5
7
3
4.1 MEGA PIXELS
FinePix
FUJINON ZOOM LENS
4
3x 5.8-17.4mm 1:2.8-4.7
8
6
2
DIGITAL CAMERA A345

A TOUR AROUND A DIGITAL COMPACT

9 Viewfinder

By looking through this you'll be able to see your subject and frame your shot.

10 Battery

This is the powerhouse of the digital compact.

11 Mode switch

Use this to switch between shooting digital stills and movies.

12 Memory

This is where your images are kept. Some memory devices are removable, others are not.

13 Zoom control

This will get you closer to the subject without having to actually move yourself. Things will appear to be enlarged in your viewfinder or LCD screen.

14 Macro mode

This is a good feature to use if you are taking close-up shots of plants or insects.

15 Flash switch

This will let you decide how much light you want thrown onto your subject. For certain shots you may decide that you don't want any flash at all.

16 LCD screen

The Liquid Crystal Display (LCD) looks like a very small TV screen. You can use it to frame your shots or play back your photos or your video footage. You will also be able to see how your camera has been set up and change it before you start shooting.

17 Menu

You can access the camera's menu by pressing this button.

VIEWING YOUR SUBJECT

With digital cameras you'll have a choice of how you want to view your subjects. With conventional cameras you would have to look through a viewfinder, but a lot of the digitals that you'll see will have a Liquid Crystal Display (LCD). These are like little television screens that are on the back of the camera. With this screen you can adjust the way the camera behaves depending on what you are photographing. The LCD will also let you see what you are about to take a picture of.

A couple of things to bear in mind are that the screen will drain your battery power, and it can be difficult to view your screen if you are in bright sunshine. It can be a bit like trying to watch a television set when the sun is streaming in through the window. You can buy little protective hoods for your LCD screen to stop this from happening.

Some cameras have adjustable LCDs, so that you'll be able to twist and turn the screen in different

LCDs in action: adjustable (above) and standard (below).

directions. These can be useful if you want to take photographs from high or low angles. The screens are also great to use when you want to scan through your shots and decide if you want to keep or delete your photos.

You may be able to view more than one image at a time. The pictures are each reduced in size and referred to as 'thumbnails'. This allows you to compare the images about nine or so at a time.

Compact camera LCDs do not show everything that the lens will capture: when you are looking at the screen you will not be looking directly through the lens. With the much more costly SLR cameras you look directly through the lens, but you can't preview your shots on the LCD with this type of camera.

SLICK MOVIES

The LCD really comes into its own when you are shooting video footage. Even if you don't intend to shoot video most of the time, it is a facility that a lot of digital cameras offer. You'll be able to play back your movie footage via the LCD.

If you're going to make a film, keep it interesting!

If you are going to be filming it is good to know how many frames per second your camera can capture. The number of frames per second determines how smooth the footage will look on the screen. The screen needs to update quickly to avoid the footage looking stilted. On average, your camera will capture about 30 frames per second, which is more than most television programmes feature!

VIEWFINDERS

There are two main types of viewfinder: one is optical and the other is electronic. The optical viewfinder is the simplest design. When you look through it to see your subject, it is a little bit like looking through a tiny telescope.

The electronic viewfinder is a miniature version of the larger LCD screen on the back of many digital cameras. It gives you a true image of what your camera is actually seeing at any given time.

Not all digital cameras have viewfinders: some of them only have an LCD screen. It's probably best to have both.

An electronic viewfinder allows you to see the true colours of your picture before taking it – perfect for sunsets.

Lens

Zoom lenses have become a popular feature on many compact digital cameras. Cheaper and more basic point-and-shoot cameras do not tend to have a zoom feature.

Luckily, robots can wander into frame themselves: no need for a zoom lens here!

Fixed Lens

This is the type of lens that you'll find on less expensive models. When you look through the viewfinder the lens will not be able to draw the subject closer to you: you will have to physically move in closer yourself. This can be inconvenient if the object of your picture is some way off.

Owing to the fact that this type of lens doesn't move, you can take photos very quickly. No time is wasted having to focus on your subject. One good thing about using a fixed lens is that it will allow you to get some much-needed exercise while you are running around chasing your subject!

ZOOMING

Most digital cameras come complete with a fancy zoom that automatically pops out of the camera. We have become used to seeing photojournalists snapping away at celebrities. They can be seen handling very large zoom lenses, also called telephoto lenses,

Not even the sneakiest celebrities can hide from a telephoto lens like this!

attempting to capture that special shot. You will be able to recreate the shots you see in glossy magazines using a digital compact with a zoom lens.

You may have noticed that cameras are advertised as having anything from a 2x zoom to a 10x zoom. Zoom lenses that have a higher number such as 8x are more powerful than ones with lower numbers, such as 2x.

Optical Zoom

This is the best type of zoom available. With this system the lens physically moves to alter the size of your subject. The quality that you get from an optical zoom is very good because the entire image will be in sharp focus. Make sure that you check whether or not the camera you choose has an optical zoom.

Optical: the only way to enlarge.

Digital Zoom

To put it simply, digital zooms are somewhat less effective. This system uses computer software in order to enlarge your subject.

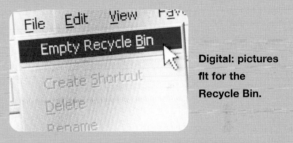

Digital: pictures flt for the Recycle Bin.

This will affect the quality of your image, because some of the pixels around the edge of your subject are discarded.

Sometimes manufacturers combine optical zooms with digital zooms in order to boost their performance, especially in the camera phone market. But if you have the option, do try to avoid cameras that feature any kind of digital zoom.

MODES

Your camera will have different modes that can be accessed via the camera's menu. The majority of menus can be viewed on the camera's LCD, which will be found on the back of the camera.

One thing to remember about digital cameras is that, like PCs or laptops, they take a while to fully switch on and become operational. It is unlikely that you will be able to turn your compact camera on and start taking photos straight away.

By going into the menu, you will be able to change the camera's settings – for example, the number of megapixels you use. In addition, you can alter the way the camera behaves depending on your subject. Don't be afraid to play around with

Portrait mode: blurred backgrounds, sharp subjects, big hotdogs.

the menu and explore what your camera is capable of doing. If you are familiar with your camera's different modes, you will be well prepared when it comes to shooting.

Your camera will already have programmes installed to suit different subjects like portraits, action and landscape shots. When your camera is set to portrait mode it will make sure that your subject is in sharp focus and the background is blurred. This is done so that when we look at the subject, we are not too distracted by the background. This is also referred to as a shallow 'depth of field'. If you are shooting fast-moving action, the sport or action setting will ensure that you don't miss your subject or produce a fuzzy image.

When you are taking pictures of wide-open spaces, you may want to select the landscape mode. This will make sure that the whole scene is in focus, not just one selected area.

Before buying a digital camera, make sure that it comes with a good range of modes. You may not use all of the features all of the time, but it's good to know that you have these features when you need them.

Landscape mode keeps everything in focus, but it can't make the sun shine!

Your picture being out of focus is not always a bad thing – it's sometimes a good thing!

KEEP FOCUSED

Focusing the lens makes your subject appear sharper in your viewfinder or LCD. The most basic point-and-shoot cameras and a lot of camera phones will not allow you to manually focus. However, the camera phone market has quickly caught up with the digital camera market and it is now possible to get phones that can be manually focused.

Most digital compacts have auto focus lenses. Modern day auto focus systems can do their job much faster than we can possibly do it manually.

Like the zoom and the viewfinder, there are two main types of auto focus systems used in digital photography – 'active' (also known as 'infrared') and 'passive'.

Active

Active auto focus relies on the camera sending out an invisible beam of light (infrared) at your chosen subject. The same light is then bounced off the subject and back to the camera, a bit like bouncing a football against a wall.

The camera uses that information – the time it takes for the light beam to return, the direction that the beam returns from and the amount of light that returns – to calculate the point of focus.

The active system doesn't require good lighting conditions in order to work properly.

Passive

This system uses a tiny CCD in order to 'see' whether the subject is in focus or not. It will then adjust the lens until the scene is in focus. Due to the way this system operates there is a possibility that it can be fooled in low light. Manufacturers do combine both the active and the passive systems in order to get the best results.

Lenses tend to focus on subjects that are in the centre of your shot or frame. If your subject is not centred you can use 'focus lock'. If your subject is off-centre, press the shutter down halfway, then point the camera at your intended subject so that it is now at the centre of the frame. Then return to the original position and take the picture.

There are some situations that can make it difficult for auto focus systems to function properly, such as if you are taking a photograph through a pane of glass or in very low light. If your auto focus is struggling, try switching to a manual override if your camera will allow it.

Infrared: the best way of focusing even in low-light photographs.

DON'T GET TOO EXPOSED

You may have heard the term 'exposure' being used a lot in connection with photography. That's because 'exposure', or rather 'light', is at the very heart of photography. No matter how technologically sophisticated our cameras are, without light in one form or another we wouldn't be able to take shots at all.

It is important that we can control the amount of light that enters the lens and hits the CCD. By restricting and adjusting the amount of light that comes into the camera, we can alter the final image. We use the aperture to control the amount of light allowed into the lens. The aperture is just a hole and, by making the hole bigger or smaller, more or less light is able to travel through the lens.

If too much light enters, our photos will be too bright or 'overexposed'. When we don't let enough light into the lens, the photos are too dark or 'underexposed'.

Luckily, just about every modern digital compact camera has a light meter that will measure the amount of light falling and bouncing off your subject.

Another great feature of a CCD is that it can automatically adjust its sensitivity. If there isn't much light available it can become more sensitive.

After measuring or 'reading' the amount of light in a given scene, the camera can then automatically adjust the shutter speed and aperture size so that the right amount of light hits the CCD.

When your camera is set to 'programme mode', your camera will calculate the right amount of light required for each shot.

Digital cameras offer different exposure modes, including:

Aperture priority – This setting will allow you to manually select the aperture while the camera sets your shutter speed.

Shutter priority – Will allow you to select the shutter speed while it selects the correct aperture.

EXPOSURE COMPENSATION

If your camera allows, don't just leave it on 'programme mode' – try out aperture and shutter priority. By selecting 'exposure compensation', you'll be able to manually adjust the exposure, allowing more or less light into the lens as and when you need it. This is particularly useful when you are shooting in difficult or unusual lighting conditions.

SHUTTER

Although the aperture controls the volume or amount of light that will get through to your CCD, the shutter determines how much time the process will last. Simply put, fast shutter speeds are best used when taking action shots. Slower shutter speeds are best used for stationary objects.

Fast shutter speeds will 'freeze' action. If you shoot a moving object with a slow shutter it will produce a blurred image.

Getting the right shutter speed is key to taking a good action shot.

The shutter can allow light to get into the lens for different amounts of time, starting at 1/1000 of a second. It is also possible to hold the shutter for minutes at a time.

'Shutter lag' used to be very common on compact digital cameras. Shutter lag was the term given to the time delay between pressing down the shutter and the shot being captured. This would happen quite often, because the electronics within the camera would take a few seconds to register the scene. Thankfully, this problem is becoming less and less common as technology improves.

LET'S GET FLASH

As you now know, light is the most important element in photography. But natural light is not always available and, even when it is, there may not be enough of it.

Even the most basic digital camera phones and compacts have built-in flash units. When the camera is in 'auto' or 'programme' mode, the flash will operate automatically if the camera doesn't think there is enough light.

Sometimes it is best to override your camera's flash – for example, when you are taking photographs through a glass window or of a reflective object, such as a shiny metal car.

Occasionally it is best to use a flash even though there is enough light to take pictures. This can be especially true on a bright sunny day. Harsh sunlight can cast unattractive shadows across people's faces. When this is the case you can select 'fill-in flash'. This will produce a low burst of light that will get rid of the dark areas in your picture.

Let there be light: master the flash, master the photograph.

With red eye mode, the 'scary look' is finally a thing of the past.

LOSE THAT RED EYE LOOK

One of the most common problems that can occur when using a flash is 'red eye'. Quite simply, your subject appears to have devilish red eyes. Apart from being quite scary, this can also make your subject look rather unattractive.

Red eye happens when the flash light bounces off the blood vessels at the back of the eye. The problem is made worse when the flash unit is too close to the camera lens.

Luckily, camera manufacturers have been attempting get rid of red eye. To overcome this, many

cameras have a 'red eye mode'. When this is activated, the flash will send out little flashes or one beam of light before the main flash is fired. This will make the subject's eyes contract or get smaller and so when the main light flashes not as much light will get through to the back of their eye.

BE PART OF THE ACTION

Thanks to the self-timer, no one needs to be left out of group shots.

There are times when, instead of just taking a picture, you'll want to be in it as well. The easiest way of doing this is to hold your camera at arm's length in front of you and take the shot. The downside to this is that, unless you have a revolving LCD, you won't be able to see what's in the frame.

If, however, you want to be part of a group shot, you could always use the 'self-timer' mode featured on many digital cameras. After selecting this mode and setting up the shot, just press the shutter: you'll then have about ten seconds to race around the camera and get into the picture.

You can use a table or a wall to balance your camera on while it snaps the photo. Just make sure it's safe when you leave it: self-timer shots are usually taken in a hurry, so be sure you've rested your camera somewhere secure and it isn't going to fall over and break in all the excitement.

POWER UP

Digital cameras need power to operate. Most cameras rely on batteries to provide this power. It is best to avoid disposable batteries and go for rechargeable, 'nickel-metal hydride' (NiMH) batteries instead.

● Don't use old batteries with new batteries and avoid mixing different brands of battery together.

● Batteries can drain very quickly in a digital camera, depending on what you are shooting. Using the LCD and shooting movies takes up a lot of power.

● Many cameras will go to sleep or into power reserve mode when they haven't been used for a while. This will save some of your power.

● One thing to remember is that even if you have fully charged your digital camera the battery will drain even while you aren't using it.

A memory hub: more cards, more shots. More money.

ACCESSORISING

There are a whole load of accessories that you can get to go along with your digital camera. Some are more useful then others: only buy the things you need.

Your camera may already come with a protective case, but if it doesn't you should definitely consider getting one. It will protect your camera from dirt, dust and minor knocks. Some cases will give your camera more protection than others depending on their padding.

A battery charger can be useful. Instead of having only one set of batteries that always remains in the camera, consider buying another set of batteries and a charger. This will mean that your picture-taking opportunities are not as restricted.

A tripod is a very underrated but valuable tool. These three-legged stands are not only useful when taking self-portraits, they can also hold your camera steady when you are taking photos in low light. This will give you a better chance of getting a clearer picture. Mini tripods are cheap and can fit in your pocket.

Smart card readers will let you download your memory card onto a computer. This means that you do not have to connect your camera up to the computer, just the card reader. Provided you have another memory card you can be free to carry on shooting while your pictures are being downloaded.

CHAPTER 3
HAPPY SNAPPING

We've looked at the camera controls and how best to use them, so now it's time for the real fun to begin. Let's get to grips with our camera and go out and shoot some photos. There are lots of excellent subjects to take photos of, and in this chapter we will be taking a look at the most popular ones. With our helpful hints and tips, you will drastically improve your results – and that's a promise!

GETTING A GRIP

Let's start by taking a look at how to hold your camera properly. You'll need to have a secure grip – this will help to make sure you don't end up with blurred shots or accidentally cutting off the tops of your pictures. That's why it is so important to choose a camera that feels comfortable in your hands. Also, if you have a camera that you feel at one with, you are much more likely to carry it around all the time and actually use it.

It's also important to hold your camera with both hands when taking a picture. If you don't, you are likely to jolt the camera as you press down on the shutter button. Remember too that when you squeeze that shutter button, you don't need to apply a lot of pressure. Thankfully, some cameras have a system called an 'image stabilizer' – this will try to compensate for any sudden movement you may make by accident. But do stay as still as possible when you click the shutter. You don't want to rely too much on technology to get you out of a tight spot at the last minute!

If for whatever reason you need extra support, you can use a mini-tripod, which is small enough to fit into your pocket. If you are out and about and you don't have a tripod to hand, then consider using a wall or tree to lean against to help keep you steady. Finally, when you are framing a shot, make sure that your fingers or the camera's straps are not dangling in front of the lens!

Your own eyes are the best judge of all.

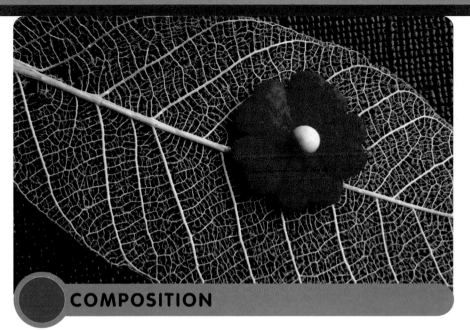

COMPOSITION

An unusual, eye-catching composition.

You may have heard this word used when people talk about photography and art. It is sometimes difficult to say what makes a good picture, but composition plays a major role.

Good composition means thinking about where you place the subject or subjects in your photograph. Is your subject close up and in clear view or is it far away in the distance? Do you want your subject to be bang in the centre of your frame or over to one side? Composition encompasses all these questions and once mastered can make your shots look brilliant.

To help you get started, take a look at photographs that you like – in books and magazines, or on posters or postcards. Then try to work out what it is about the pictures that you really like. Is it the lighting, the colours, or the position of the people or buildings? Is it what the people are wearing or just the people themselves? Perhaps it's the way the picture is composed – in other words, how the subject of the photograph is placed.

Like the term 'composition', 'rule of thirds' also crops up a lot in photography and art. This is a method that is sometimes used to determine the best place to 'put' the subject within the frame. When we start taking pictures, we all tend to put our subjects squarely in the centre of the frame. The 'rule of thirds' simply means that the main subjects are slightly off centre to create a more interesting composition. Experiment for yourself and see what you think.

PEOPLE PICTURES

The Basics

By far the most popular photos taken are 'people pictures' or 'portraits'. We never ever seem to get bored of taking or looking at pictures of each other. One of the reasons why portraits are so popular is because of the subjects – people are so accessible because we're surrounded by them! Tall, short, wide, thin, dark or fair: think about all of the people you know, and think how different they all are.

Most people enjoy seeing photos that make them look good, so if you manage to do that, you won't ever be short of models, and your digital camera can help you in the pursuit of the perfect portrait. Your camera has a special mode designed for taking decent photos of people; it will be called 'portrait' or 'tele' mode.

When you put your camera into this mode, it means that when you focus in on your subject, the background will normally be thrown out of focus, with the subject in focus. This is great

because, when we look at the picture, our eyes will naturally be drawn to the main subject – the person or people. Remember, it's not good to have things that will distract the viewer or get in the way of our main subject.

It's standard practice for photographers to focus in on the subject's eyes; after all, it is often said that 'the eyes are the windows of the soul'. This is good advice; but don't think that the person has to be looking directly down the lens for the result to be a good shot.

Say cheese! Snap a good portrait and it'll be smiles all round.

There are also no rules about how much of the subject you should get in your frame. You could go for a tight head shot – this will mean that you only include the person's head and possibly shoulders. Or perhaps you might prefer a mid- or 3/4-length shot that will reveal some of the clothes that your subject is wearing. Maybe a full-length portrait would be more appropriate, which will show the whole person from head to toe. Not quite sure? One thing to remember is that you can always cut or crop your picture at a later stage – see page 102.

PEOPLE PICTURES

Portrait Ideas

1 Capture the character!

Clever photographers can 'capture' something about the person they are photographing. The photos can say something about the subject's personality – they can be serious, funny, happy or sad. The majority of portraits that you take are most likely going to be of friends and family. You'll know them very well, but can you capture their personality in a photo?

Try different locations to take your portraits.

2 Walk the walk

Some of your friends may be very fashion conscious and you could highlight this by paying particular attention to a certain aspect of their clothing. Maybe their hat or their trainers could add interest to your picture and say something about your subject.

From the hatwalk to the catwalk.

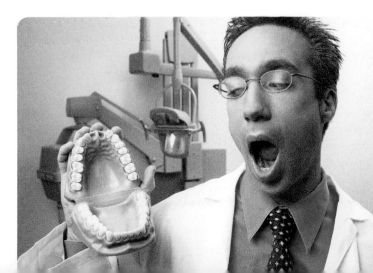

3 All in a day's work

You can tell a lot about a person by what they wear – you may be able to tell what they do for a living. They could be a teacher, police officer, fire fighter … or the dreaded dentist! Think about all the different uniforms you see every day to and from school. Do you see any unusual or interesting uniforms that you could take a photograph of?

PEOPLE PICTURES

Groups

It can be difficult to take a picture of a large or even a small group – sometimes a group just standing around can look messy. There are several ways to help you get the best group shot though. It's often a good idea to set your camera to landscape mode so that no one in the picture appears out of focus.

When you are arranging a group, make sure that you can see everybody's face and keep everyone tightly together. Check your playback to make sure that everyone was looking at the camera with their eyes open when you took the shot – there's always someone who isn't! Of course, the great thing about digital is that you can delete a shot that doesn't work and then take it again.

In order to make sure that the entire group is looking at you at the same time, you can count out loud backwards from three to one. This way everyone will know exactly when to expect the shutter to fire.

1 Row by row

You don't have to have everyone standing in one line – you could have a couple of lines, one in front of the other. This can be a much more interesting composition than one long line, and you can put shorter people at the front and much taller people at the back.

2 Sitting down to attention

Sometimes, the informal look is best – especially when dealing with friends and family. Try having everyone sitting down, huddled in a cosy semi-circle. This can create a much more informal and family-like effect – plus your photo could end up out on display in the living room for all visitors to see!

3 All together now!

Remember, there are no hard-and-fast rules when it comes to group shots. Sometimes, it can be best to have a mixture of people sitting, crouching and kneeling in your photograph. If the group is not getting too bored, try taking a few shots in different set-ups, and then you can decide which ones look better at a later date.

TOP PORTRAIT TIPS

● Make sure that your subject fills your frame: if your zoom lens can't take you close enough, physically move in closer yourself.

● Not paying attention to the background is one of the things that a lot of us are guilty of when we get caught up in the excitement of taking a photo. So be extra aware – you don't want the background to detract from the subject!

● Try to have clean, uncluttered backgrounds: bright colours, lights, trees and lamp posts can all spoil a good picture.

● Check to make sure there isn't a strange object 'growing' out of your subject's head like a light or a tree branch in the background!

● Think about whether it is best to take the picture horizontally or vertically (landscape or portrait format). If you are not sure, take the shot both ways and decide later.

● When you are taking a picture of someone who is shorter then you, get down to their level. You should also do this if your subject is sitting down. Matching their eye level will make for a better angle and shot.

● When you have checked the background, check out the foreground. Unattractive objects such as litter will not add to the quality of the shot.

● If there are dark shadows or lines across your subject's face, use the fill-in flash mode. If that doesn't improve things, move your subject to a completely different location.

● You'll get better results from your subject if they are relaxed in your company. This won't be a problem if you are taking shots of friends and family. However, if it's a new subject, some time spent explaining what you want to capture will help ease them into giving you the best results.

LOCATION, LOCATION, LOCATION

The Basics

There are lots of places around us that will make excellent locations for your photos. You'll find that they are places we use every day without thinking about them. Think about all the places you have visited over the past week – have you been to school, visited a local park, a playground, or perhaps travelled even further?

You don't have to go abroad or be on holiday to find good locations. Look closer to home, and use the objects and structures that surround you. If you are lucky enough to have a garden, why not see if it could be used as either a backdrop for a portrait or the subject of a photograph. It doesn't have to be summertime either: after all, colourful brown and red autumn leaves can look even better than lush green ones.

Landscape has long been a very popular photographic subject, and like portraiture it can either be formal or informal. Formal landscapes express a 'mood' or 'impression' of a place and are often similar to or based on many of the classic pictures painted by great artists now hanging in art galleries around the world. It's partly because of this that when we think of 'landscape', a lot of us naturally imagine rolling fields, but urban landscapes or cityscapes can also give sometimes spectacular and unexpected results.

Keep your eyes peeled: the least likely places often make the most spectacular shots!

LANDSCAPE IDEAS

1 Playtime

Playgrounds can provide you with a good setting. If you're taking pictures of your friends, put them on the swings or the roundabouts. Click away as they swing back and forth or spin around. You can also use climbing frames and objects to actually frame your subjects.

2 "I'm in a good mode!"

Your camera should have a landscape mode on it. By selecting this mode, your camera will choose a medium to slow shutter speed depending on the available light. It will also select a smaller aperture to allow a wide depth of field. All this really means is that the fore, mid and background will all be in focus.

3 Focus

One of the mistakes that many of us make when taking a landscape shot is to try and cram too much into a single frame. Next time you see a landscape scene, look across it, take it all in, and then pick out one specific area of interest. You can then use this as the focal point of your picture.

4 A tale of four seasons

When you are taking landscape shots in a 'natural' setting instead of an urban one, seasonal changes will make a difference to your results. For example, there tends to be less foliage during winter months and this could make your pictures look a bit sparse. In an urban setting, seasonal changes may not have as much of an effect. However, even the look of a city changes depending on the time of day.

TOP LOCATION TIPS

● See how the same scene changes as time passes. You'll be amazed at the difference light can make to a landscape, even during different times of the day, never mind night!

● Remember to always look for a focal point that will become the 'highlight' of your photo.

● Use easily accessible locations and always make sure you let your parents know where you are going. If you do want to go somewhere out of the ordinary, it would be a good idea to get them to come along with you, just to be safe.

- Don't forget to set your camera to 'landscape mode'. That mode is there to make your life easier.

- Take a spare memory card with you when you go out so you don't end up being frustrated because you ran out of memory space on your camera.

- Always take a mobile phone with you so you can make a phone call if you find yourself in a situation you are not happy with.

- Don't trespass, or ever put yourself in danger in order to take a photograph.

- Always take your camera with you when you go out – you never know when you might come across a possible picture to take!

ANIMAL MAGIC

Taking pictures of your pets could help you to improve your photographic skills. This is because animals can be difficult to photograph, taking a lot of time and patience on your part. As with all aspects of good photography, preparation and practice will bring their rewards.

Cats and dogs are by far the most popular choice for many photographers. You have probably seen cute kittens or puppies featured on calendars. One of the difficulties that you

may find is that the animal simply does not want to cooperate with your wishes and would rather not take part in your photoshoot.

However, there are a few tricks that you can use to improve your chances of getting the best shot. If you're trying to take photos of your lively or over-excitable dog, but want to do so when it is slightly more calm and relaxed, take the animal on a long walk before you begin shooting. It should use up some of your pet's excess energy!

As with humans, animals look best in their natural environment. It's good to see an animal outdoors. This does not only apply to larger pets like dogs and cats, but also smaller pets such as rabbits or hamsters. If you do decide to go outside, make sure that the area is secure so that your pet can't bound off or slip away under the garden fence and begin eating your neighbour's tulips! If you have an outside run for your pet, get inside it with the animal – it will make for a better shot than shooting through the wire mesh of a cage.

Man's best friend is
on pretty good terms
with his camera, too.

ANIMAL IDEAS

1 Prepare that pet!

Before you start taking pictures of your pet, whether it is a cat, dog, budgie or pony, make sure it is looking its best. This could mean just giving it a light brush or setting up a bath. As you will no doubt know, some animals react better to being cleaned than others. Just do what you can to make the animal look presentable. With dogs, pay particular attention to their drooling jaws: this is definitely not a good look!

2 Pick your spot

Put a bit of thought into where you want to take the shot. Will it be indoors or outdoors? An outdoor shot may look more natural, and could mean that you don't need to use a flash. If possible, avoid using flash because this could upset your pet. As with human portraits, get down (or up) to their eye level. This is easy to do if you are photographing a hamster or kitten, but not so easy if you have a pet giraffe. Lucky you!

3 Off the leash

Sometimes it is good to keep your pet occupied while you are taking pictures. This can be easily done by giving your animal a favourite toy or ball to play with. However, if your pet is running around, you will have to select an 'action' or 'sport' mode on your camera. This will enable your camera to keep up with your pet! A good rule of thumb is to follow your pet through your viewfinder or on your LCD and try to anticipate your animal's movements. Take as many shots as you can in order to get a good picture. If possible, only let your pet run around in a limited space. You don't really want to miss shots because you have to traipse miles across fields!

SPORTS SHOTS

You can get some great shots on the sports field, and you don't need to have a season ticket to the big games either! Look for sporting venues that are easily accessible to you – for example, why not take your camera along to your next school sports day? You will have a variety of sports to choose from and entry will be free.

The most successful sports photographers know a lot about the sports they shoot, and you will find it very useful if you understand the way a game or event works. If you know where most of the action is going to take place, you'll be able to anticipate it! For example, soccer photographers often favour being near the goal in order to capture a striker's talents as they kick a ball into the back of the net!

If you learn a sport properly, this will mean that you could be perfectly positioned to be in the right place at the right time – and get the very best shot possible!

Making sure that your camera is well prepared is one thing, but make sure that you are as well. It is a good idea to travel light if you are planning on running up and down a touch line. If you don't want to be weighed down with a bag, wear trousers or a jacket with lots of different compartments or pockets. It's best if they can be buttoned down or zipped up to stop things from falling out. As well as keeping any accessories such as spare batteries safe, don't forget to take a tasty snack as a half-time treat too!

"Okay, now hold that pose. Hold it... hold it..."

SPORTS IDEAS

1 Panning

If your camera will allow you, try to pre-focus your view in the area that you think the action will happen. If not, you can use a technique called panning. This is simply where you follow the movement through a viewfinder, swivelling the top half of your body from left to right and vice versa. Try not to make any jerky movements – you need to aim for a smooth flow.

2 Keeping your eye off the ball

Don't always look at a game in the same way an ordinary spectator would. For example, when we look at a match we all tend to follow the ball. Our eyes naturally go wherever the ball is, but something worth trying is to follow one player. Keep your camera on a particular player even when they are not in possession of the ball – this is a good method to use for tennis matches.

3 Press gang

There are lots of local teams and maybe even your own school team that would appreciate their own official photographer. If you become good at taking sports shots, you can cover all of their home games. Depending on how successful your team becomes, the local newspaper may even be interested in printing the pictures.

BUILDINGS

There are a lot of buildings that we see or use every day that we take for granted. People who specialise in taking pictures of buildings are called architectural photographers. Why not give it a go yourself? Take a closer look at the buildings you pass every day or so – do you notice anything special about them? Do you know what the building is used for? Some buildings are purpose-built, like churches and railway stations, while others could be used for just about anything – it may only be a sign across the front that gives any clue about the building's use. You needn't venture far, either – take a look at your own home. Is it a house, a flat or a bungalow? Is there anything that makes your home different from your neighbours'? If so, then you could take your first building photograph right on your own front doorstep!

When you are out and about in search of new or unusual buildings in an unfamiliar area, take a pen and paper with you so that you can write down its location. Also, make a note of the time of day you took the shot – this information will appear on your image, but may vanish when you transfer it. This is particularly handy when taking shots of glass structures, because they can look different depending on the time of day. Also, look out for other buildings from which to take shots. Maybe shoot through an archway or doorway opposite your subject and use this to frame your shot of the building.

A familiar place can look like a different planet after sunset.

BUILDING IDEAS

1 Grand design

Countries the world over are filled with interesting and grand architecture, but you don't just have to look at old or traditional buildings to find a great shot. There are a lot of new buildings going up every month that are worthy of a shot or two. Glass office buildings are quite popular with designers at the moment and they can present good opportunities for a photographer. See how these buildings reflect the scene around them. The outside world looks like it is being screened on the walls of the building itself!

2 Gaze skyward

Look up when you are walking along next time! Many of us spend too much time looking down and missing great architecture. If a building does catch your eye, take a look at it from another angle if possible. Try to select a small detail that says something about the building or the people inside it.

3 History of the future

Looking at old pictures of your local area will give you a good idea of how the area has changed over the years. Your modern-day pictures of buildings could provide an archive for children in the future.

LESSONS IN LIGHT

What a difference a day makes: slight changes in light make for truly striking pictures, as in these shots of London.

Make the most of daylight. There's lots of it and it's free. Natural light is a wonderful tool. Have you noticed how it changes at different times of the day? If you get up very early in the morning, you may notice that the light is 'cold' and has a hint of blue in it. The midday sun on a summer's day is high in the sky and will be at its brightest. At the end of the day, there is an orange or yellowy glow in the sky.

As an exercise, select one room in your house and see how the sunlight moves around the room during the day. Photograph it. Notice how shadows on the walls become longer and shorter during the course of a day.

SHOOTING AT NIGHT

Night time can provide you with some really stunning shots. Normally the most obvious thing that you will need if you are shooting at night is a flash – it is true that a flash will be able to throw light onto a scene so that you can capture a photograph in darkness. Do bear in mind though that sometimes it is best to switch off your flash. Set your camera to the 'fireworks' or 'night' mode and see what results it produces.

When you are taking pictures at night, the camera needs to make use of all the available light. In order to do this and make the most of the situation, it will need a slow shutter speed. Unfortunately a slow shutter speed means that you will have to hold the camera very steady – if you

don't, your picture might come out blurred or, worse still, it might not come out at all!

If you are serious about taking photos at night, it may well be worth buying a tripod so you can take the perfect night-time shot!

Capturing fireworks takes skill, but do it well and you can almost hear the bang!

CHAPTER 4
HOOKING UP

So now that you have taken lots of shots and your camera's memory is full, you'll have to think about what to do with them. In this chapter, you're going to learn the best ways of using those amazing pictures you have taken.

From downloading them onto your home computer through to emailing them onto friends and family: in no time at all, you will learn how to build a brilliant collection of your best photographs for everyone to enjoy!

DOWNLOADING YOUR MOBILE PHONE PICTURES

Downloading your pictures from a camera phone varies depending on the make and model that you have. If your camera has a removable memory device, then your life will be much easier. However, if like many mobile phones yours has an onboard memory, it may not be quite so simple.

You may have to buy some synching software, complete with a cable, so that you can connect the phone to a computer or laptop. One end of the cable will fit into your phone-charging socket, while the other end will plug straight into a computer.

Your computer will have a Universal Serial Bus (USB) port, but your phone may not. And even

Store images on CD for safe-keeping.

if it does have a USB connection, it may not be the same size as the one on your computer! Ask in the shop if you're confused.

More and more phones are being fitted with wireless connections such as 'Bluetooth'. Wireless allows you to link two or more pieces of hardware together without using troublesome wires or cables. You should also bear in mind what the operating system or platform your computer uses if you are transferring pictures. As always, make sure that any software you buy is compatible with your system, whether it's 'Windows' or 'Apple Mac'. All of this may seem like a lot of hassle, but it's simple once you've set it up the first time.

Another popular printing option all over the world is to use a photo kiosk, which lets you connect your phone to a machine for print outs.

Another method is to transfer your images using the internet. You can save your photos and send them as a picture message to an email account if your phone has WAP (Wireless Application Protocol). WAP allows mobile devices such as phones to connect directly to the internet.

Email accounts are very fast and easy to set up and some are free, such as those provided by Yahoo and Hotmail. You should get a parent or guardian to open an account on your behalf. When you have your email account, you'll be able to send your pictures to yourself and download them.

BLUETOOTH

The Bluetooth process is really very simple:

● Go into your phone's menu to enable your Bluetooth technology.

● Stand close to the kiosk: wireless devices have a limited range.

● Search on your mobile phone's menu to look for Bluetooth devices. This should appear as 'kiosk' or something similar on your phone. You will now be able to download your photos immediately and directly.

DOWNLOADING FROM YOUR DIGITAL CAMERA

View your images on your very own television set.

The LCD on the back of digital cameras is often described as a mini TV set, but how about viewing your photos on a real TV? If your TV can be linked to a DVD player, it can be linked to a digital camera. Your digital camera may have come with an AV connecting cable. You can use this to play your video and stills photos on your TV. This isn't strictly a method of downloading – it is just a good way of viewing your images.

There are a few ways that you can download your photos. Your camera kit should include a USB cable and a 'driver' in the form of a CD. However, depending on how old your computer system is, you may not need to install any additional software.

A simple wire can hook your photos up to your PC and open up a whole new world.

The 'Windows' operating system will be able to transfer your digital photos using the 'Scanner and Camera Wizard'. When you have downloaded your photos, make sure that you label them so that you can easily find them when you want to. It is really important that

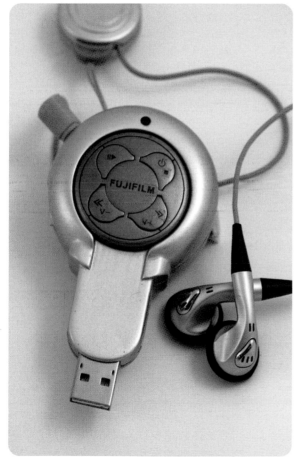

you save your photographs in files and folders so group shots are together, or you could list the shots taken at a certain time. You could group all of your holiday photographs together under 'Summer Holiday 2006'. Then you can name each individual shot: eg 'red sunset', 'skiing' or even 'me riding a horse'.

It's also possible to download with a smart card reader. You can slide your memory card into these little devices then plug it into a laptop or PC. You'll then be able to download your images.

Another way of downloading your images is to go to a photo shop and let them do it for you. Over the last couple of years, there has been an increase in the number of digital photographic services available. Most of these shops just need you to bring your camera's memory card along and they will download it for you – they will also be able to edit your prints if you want them to. It's a great and convenient service to use occasionally, but it will work out easier and cheaper to do it yourself in the long run.

Memory card readers come in all shapes and sizes – this one is also an MP3 player.

EMAILING

The first ever email message was 'QWERTYUIOP' (the first row of letters on a keyboard), and was sent twenty-five years ago. Things have moved on a great deal since then and today we transfer photos, files and documents via electronic mail.

Emailing photos will let you download them onto an alternative computer system, share your pictures with all your friends and store them on a cyber gallery for easy access.

If you are planning to email images, it is best to check how much data your email account will allow you to store. Photos can take up a lot of

SENDING A PHOTO VIA EMAIL

● Sending a photo email is similar to sending a text-only message. Click on the 'create' button to begin and enter the email address of the person that you wish to send the photos to.

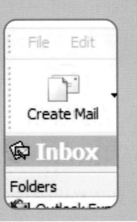

● You can send photos as an 'attachment'. To do so, click on 'attachment'. By doing this, you will be taken to a new page. Here you can click on a 'browse' button. When you click on 'browse', you will be able to access all of the files on your computer. Click on 'My Pictures' to locate your desired photo file.

space, so it is best to check how many GBs (gigabytes) your account will let you store on it.

It is because of limited space and the amount of time photos take to download that it is best to transfer smaller or compressed files like JPEGs instead of larger ones.

● When you have found your photo in the 'My Pictures' folder, click on the photo that you wish to attach and this will open the file. Now this is the time when you will be glad that you have labelled each of your photos. You may not be able to view the photograph: you may only be able to see an icon and the picture's title.

● After you have clicked on the photo, its title will appear in a 'letter box'. Underneath that, the picture's file format is displayed. This may be JPEG, TIFF etc. Click on 'attach' and then 'continue to message' in order to get back to the email compose page. Attachments are limited by size, and depending on the size of your file, you will be able to attach five or six attachments to each individual email.

WONDERFUL WORLD WIDE WEB

The internet has changed the world around us forever.

You may not have heard of Tim Berners-Lee, but you will know his invention, the 'World Wide Web'. The British scientist invented the 'www' in 1989, and ever since it has had a big impact on the way that we get and view information.

The internet is made up of millions of computers that are linked together, and which can exchange information with one another.

All of the data, photo files and so on that go into making a website are stored on computer hard drives. These computers are permanently connected to the internet and referred to as 'web servers'. But unlike the computers that we use at

Get your own website and before long the whole world will be watching.

home, these computers allow anyone to access them. We can do this by using a 'web browser'.

Most of us surf web pages by paying a monthly subscription to an Internet Service Provider (ISP). There are lots of them around which you may have heard of, such as AOL.

Having your own website is a great way to display your work so that other people can also admire your efforts. If you are planning to create your own website, one of the big questions for you will be: 'Who will host it?' Well, luckily you do not have to spend thousands of pounds on computer hardware to get everything in place.

Some ISPs will host your personal site for free if you are already a customer. On these sites, you will be able to use some basic web design software and 'templates' in order to build your own website.

You'll be able to select different colours and text styles for your homepage. You can also have links added and use icons like the pictures available from clipart websites to brighten it up.

BLOGGING

"Dear Diary... today I started my very own blog!"

Have you ever blogged? Would you like to, or don't you have a clue what the word means? The word 'blog' comes from 'weblog'. The first blogs appeared in 1994 and were really just online diaries. People, mainly journalists, would write their day-to-day thoughts on the web for everyone to read. Since that time blogs have become more popular as more of us get easier access to the internet. A lot of bloggers group together with others who have similar interests: you'll see a community of online bloggers who may have an interest in a particular hobby, pastime or even band. Most blogs will consist of a title, date, the main text or pictures and summaries of previous blogs. Some blog pages allow readers to leave comments and have links to other bloggers and websites. There are dedicated 'blog hosting sites' and 'blog software' to help get you started. 'Tripod', 'AOL' and 'Yahoo' all provide services for bloggers. Because blogs are just other people's personal thoughts, the amount of interesting topics varies greatly – from the truly boring to the totally riveting. There are things that you can do to make your blog stand out from the millions of others out there – it just takes a little experimentation. At the end of the day, the most fascinating thing about blogs is the insight they offer into the lives of ordinary people like yourself. Try writing one – you could end up famous!

ONLINE SAFETY

The internet is a wonderful invention, but it is important to use some basic common sense when you are online.

You should not give out any personal details about yourself to strangers. Don't disclose your surname, school, address, mobile or home phone number or even the places you like to go to with your friends. You cannot be sure what other people will do with this information. Any information that you give out over the internet is potentially available to the entire world. Here are some other top tips:

● Don't agree to meet someone you've met online in person. Although they may seem okay, you don't really know them.

● If you receive files or attachments from people you don't know, think twice before opening them – they may contain viruses that could infect or crash your computer system.

● We should all be able to use the internet to have fun safely. But occasionally this is not the case, so if you receive any messages, emails or photographs that make you feel unhappy or uncomfortable, tell a parent or guardian immediately.

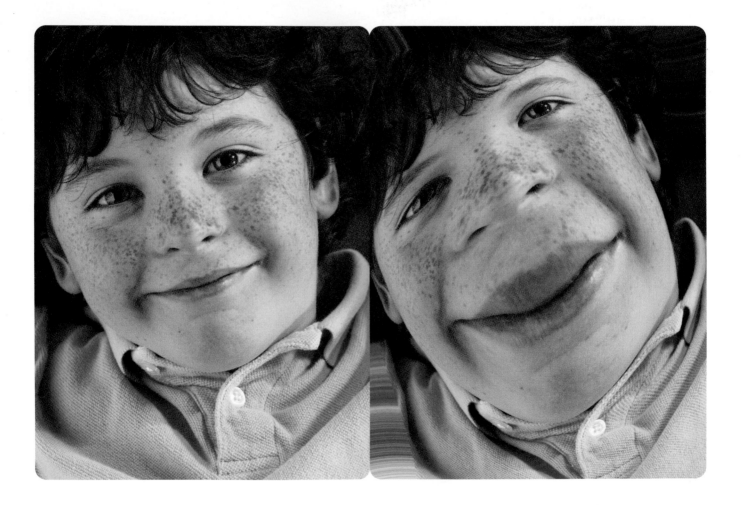

CHAPTER 5
DIGITAL WIZARDRY

In the old days, we just had to settle for the pictures we took, so we were sometimes lumbered with poor prints and had no chance to correct things. When photographs were airbrushed, this would be a lengthy and costly business limited to commercial photographers. Digital photography has changed all of that forever. In this chapter, we take a look at editing your photos. But there is one important rule to bear in mind for any real photographer – do your best to edit your photograph before you even click the shutter. That is the sign of a true photographer!

GETTING STARTED

There is lots of digital editing software available: many digital cameras and scanners and most computers already have some installed on it. So the likelihood is that your PC or Mac already has what you need to get started. If you can't find any sort of photo editor on your system, there are a few packages that you can download from the internet for free. The most popular software packages on the market include: Adobe Photoshop Elements, Jasc Paint Shop, Windows XP Media Center, Roxio and Serif.

Set up your screen

Before you start editing your photos on your computer, you have to make sure that the images you see on your computer monitor accurately show the pictures you have taken. The process for doing this is known as calibration. This can also be carried out on your printer so that the colours in your picture are the same as the ones that get printed. You can get software that will show you how to calibrate your monitor.

There are many software packages on the market to help you store and edit your images.

The ultimate edit

We have already looked at the benefits of accurately labelling your photographs. You will appreciate the time you can save by quickly and easily finding your valuable shots. But before you embark on spending time and effort editing, decide whether or not it is worth it. Delete the bad or just plain boring photographs, shots that cannot be improved with any amount of technical toys.

Old-fashioned slides can be bulky and delicate to store – but digital images saved onto a CD can be stored with ease.

Save originals

Things don't always go to plan: you may edit some photos and not be happy with the results, so always make sure that you keep a copy of the original. You will then be able to have another go some other time. It is also good if you can save copies of your photos at different stages of the editing process, so if you have a complicated edit in mind or make a mistake, you won't always have to start from scratch.

CROPPING

Sometimes the best way to improve a photograph is simply to get rid of part of it. Cropping just means cutting part of your photo – it may sound drastic, but there are times when this is your best option. You may have taken a good photo that has a distracting object in the foreground or background such as a signpost, a tree or even your stray finger-tip sneaking in front of the lens.

Instead of removing it using any other method, cropping your picture can be best. Or you may have a blank, boring area on one side of your picture that does not add anything at all to your photograph. Another good reason for cropping is to add impact to a photo. This can make an average picture into a much more powerful one. Another benefit of cropping is that you will be able to change your photo from one format to another – so you can go from portrait to landscape in an instant with the press of a button.

Before cropping.

After cropping.

BRIGHTNESS AND CONTRAST

... so lighten it using your picture editing software.

The original image is too dark...

We have all taken pictures that are too light or too dark. This can happen as a result of selecting the wrong light exposure for the scene or if an image is poorly scanned. To correct this we can adjust the brightness and the contrast, so that the image appears lighter. Contrast refers to the 'tonal range' and affects how dark the shadows will appear in the image. Just about every basic software programme will let you change the brightness and contrast, and most will allow it to be done automatically.

CLONING – NOW YOU SEE IT, NOW YOU DON'T

So far we have looked at small editing techniques that you can use to enhance your photos. Now let's take a look at one of the most exciting and most dramatic aspects of digital photography – 'cloning'. This tool is not only used to hide blemishes, it can also remove large parts of a photo completely. You'll be able to cut out anything from a whole building to a small tree. This is similar to the cut and paste facility that you have probably used when writing text documents. Cloning is particularly good if you want to cover a spot or a blemish on a model's face. It's usually much easier to

clone your picture than go and re-shoot the photo all over again to 'repair' a fault. If you are removing an object

Before cloning.

from a photo you will be left with a hole. One of the magical things about this tool is that it can take a sample

copy from a different area of the picture and use it to 'fill' the hole. One of the things that you have to consider

when making a clone is to use a sample that will match the original area's colour and lighting convincingly.

After cloning.

SHARPEN THE SHOT

Before sharpening.

After sharpening.

Most software will have a 'sharpening filter'. This tool will allow you to sharpen up a slightly soft or out-of-focus image. It is quite an amazing trick, but be warned: it cannot turn your badly out-of-focus shots into pin sharp ones. What it can do is make the edges of your subject slightly clearer and increase the contrast between the subject and its background. It is possible to overdo the sharpening and be left with unsatisfactory results on your monitor, but what appears to be over-sharpened on screen can look better in print. It's good to do a bit of experimenting with this tool to get the best results from it.

ADDING BLUR

After adding blur.

Before adding blur.

You may be wondering why, when so much effort is put into creating clear and non-blurred images, we should use a tool that actually adds blur. Well you're right, unintentional blurring is bad. But there are occasions when adding a bit of blur to an action shot will actually improve it. By selecting the action or sport modes on your digital camera, the shutter speed is increased so that the action is frozen. Sometimes a bit of blurring can add 'movement' to a photo and make it more interesting. Also, it is difficult to judge how much blurring will occur when you take an action shot, so it can be better to have a 'clean' shot and add some blurring at the editing stage.

Before adjusting colour.

After adjusting colour.

CONTROLLING COLOUR

Editing software will allow you to give your colours extra punch! Occasionally you will find that the colours in your picture don't reflect what you saw at the time. Your digital camera uses 'white balance' in order to truly represent the colours we see. Colours are measured in 'temperatures' on what is called the 'Kelvin Scale'; these temperature readings are taken through the lens. Your camera will automatically adjust the red, green and blue colours that it 'sees' after it has measured them using the white balance. When this white balance doesn't properly read the colours, it is possible to correct the fault with editing software. You'll be able to add or remove colour from your photo using a sliding scale or a dial at the editing stage.

BLACK AND WHITE

Before adjustment.

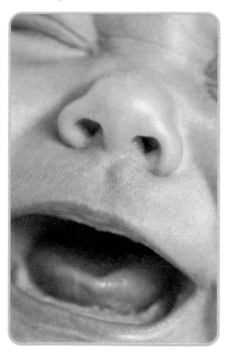

After adjustment.

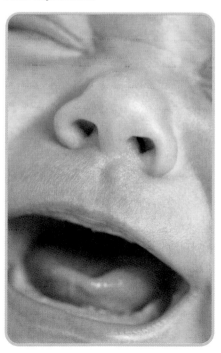

There are some photos that can look better in black and white. The colours in an image can distract the eye from noticing certain details or patterns. By removing the colour in a photograph our eyes can concentrate more on the form and shape of a picture. There was a time when all photographs were produced in black and white and now this method is becoming popular again, particularly in portraits. One of the advantages in producing black and white or 'monochrome' images is that uneven or blotchy skin tones do not show up as much as they would in colour shots. This is particularly useful if you are photographing your spotty brother or sister! Don't forget to keep a copy of the original photo because you won't be able to put the colour back once you've lost it.

DODGING AND BURNING

Now this may sound like a new X-Box game, but it isn't. It's what you do if you want to lighten and darken certain parts of your photos. To 'dodge and burn' in photographic terms is a way in which you can increase and decrease the light and shadows in specific areas of a photo. There are times when you don't want to brighten or darken the whole photo; perhaps you simply want to lighten your subject's face so that it stands out more clearly from the background.

Remember – dodge refers to lightening, while burning means to darken. In the pictures here, the girl's face has been darkened slightly – so the image has technically been 'burnt'!

Before dodge and burning.

After dodge and burning.

THE CAMERA NEVER LIES!

It is said that 'the camera never lies'. There may be some truth in that but, by using image manipulation special effects, we can certainly bend the truth. This is possibly one of the most distinctive and unique things about digital imaging. Seeing a photograph that bears no resemblance to the original image that you saw through your viewfinder or on your LCD is very exciting. It allows us to create scenes that are total fantasy and that we could never reproduce in real life.

We mainly use editing software to 'improve' on reality by slightly altering what's already in the frame. However, there may be times when you are after an extreme, fantastic or completely over the top image, perhaps in order to illustrate some school coursework.

Before manipulating.

All editing software comes with some degree of special effects, and some are more advanced than others. Using 'distortion' techniques is a popular and fun trick to play on your

After manipulating.

computer. Your software may allow you to select various forms of distortion from the 'special effects' menu on your image bar. There are different forms of distortion available including 'ripple', 'pinch and punch' and 'wave'. All of these will distort your photos in various ways. You can control the amount or intensity of each distortion by using sliding bars so that you get the effect you want. As always, don't forget to save the originals, just in case.

MONTAGE

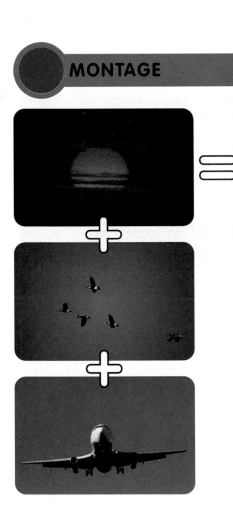

Create montages from a selection of your pictures.

Creating a 'montage' – sometimes referred to as 'collage' – is a very popular technique that has been used by artists for many, many years. You may have made collages yourself at school. The traditional way of making a collage was to cut pictures out of a magazine or newspaper and stick them together on another piece of paper. By adding these photos together, you can build up a completely new image.

You can do exactly the same and with an even smoother finish using editing software. Try to select a fairly bland background so that it doesn't interfere or detract from the pictures that you add. The results tend not to be as slick as the image you'd get if you just worked with layers. Search for 'collage', 'montage' and 'insert' to experiment with this technique.

Filters are used in both digital and conventional photography regularly. In conventional photography, filters – which are just thin pieces of glass or plastic that are fitted onto the front of the lens – are used to enhance a photo. They come in different colours and provide various effects, such as providing a warm orange glow to a dull sky. With digital photography there is less of a need to use filters at the picture-taking stage, because you can get the same results later on.

The filters that come with your software will enable you to create some unusual effects. By going into your image menu and searching for 'filters' or 'filter effects' you'll get access to a range of useful tricks. There are filters that 'multiply', 'dissolve', 'solarize' 'soften' or turn your image into a mosaic. You'll be able to change the very texture of your pictures by using these incredible applications.

FILTER EFFECTS

Before using the 'solarize' filter.

After using the 'solarize' filter.

CHAPTER 6
PERFECT PRINTS

Printing photos from conventional film was a complicated and time-consuming task involving specialist equipment. Today, with digital photography, the process couldn't be more simple. More of us are starting to print our own pictures at home. This is a good thing because, until recently, most digital photographers didn't bother printing their results. It is exciting to be able to actually hold an image after you've only previously seen it on a screen. Don't worry if you don't have a printer or access to one. There are other options available to you, which we will look at later on.

PRINTERS

Most of us will use 'inkjet' printers to produce our digital pictures. They are a common sight and will usually come as part of a standard home PC package.

Printers come in various shapes and sizes. The majority of domestic printers will be able to produce pictures that are roughly the same size as an A4 sheet. Some printers can also accept larger paper sizes so that you could produce A3-sized pictures. However, some industrial printers are capable of producing posters a couple of metres long!

These printers are very versatile and can produce good quality photos and text. Inkjet printers operate by squirting millions of tiny drops of ink onto the paper one line at a time, gradually creating a whole picture. They can produce over 16 million different colour combinations.

If your computer does not already come with a printer, make sure that any printer you buy can be used with your computer. Printers can be linked up to a computer using a Universal Serial Bus (USB) port or by using a wireless connection such as Bluetooth.

A world of colour awaits.

COLOUR

The majority of printers will have two separate cartridges; one will have black ink whilst the other will have colours. Although you can get printers with four different colours – cyan, magenta, yellow and black – it is best to get one that has five or six separate colours.

PICTURE QUALITY

Quality cartridges are vital to prints.

The quality of printers is measured in 'dots per square inch' (dpi). The higher the dpi, the better your image quality will be. A 2400dpi print will look better than a photograph printed using a 1200dpi printer. 'Resolution' is the measure of image quality: the higher the resolution, the better the quality.

When you buy a new printer, it will come with a 'driver'. This will most likely be in the form of a CD. This CD contains a lot of information about the printer, such as make and model.

The CD will guide you through the process of installing this new piece of hardware. The 'Windows' system uses the 'Wizard' to help you through the process.

The computer needs to be able to 'speak' to the printer in order to give it instructions about the prints you want to produce.

PRINTING

When you have downloaded your photos onto a computer, you can then begin the process of printing. Here are the basic steps:

1 Your pictures should be downloaded into a picture file or folder. It may appear as 'My Pictures' on a 'Windows' system. It's here that you will see all of the photos in your file.

2 Click on your desired picture to highlight it. It will appear in a small preview box. Click on the 'Full Screen Preview' so that you can see an enlarged version of the photograph. The photo will now be displayed in a larger form so that you can check the photograph up close. When you're happy, click on the 'Print' icon. But there are other options available before finishing.

3 While your picture is open instead of going straight to printing, you can click on 'File' and scroll down to 'Print'. By opening the print dialogue box you can set the printer up for the type of paper and photo size that you require. Here you can also select the number of copies you want to make. Choose wisely – printing photos eats ink and ink cartridges cost!

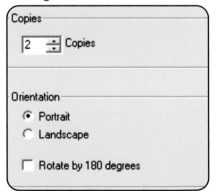

4 'Orientation' is another term that you will see here. You will be able to select either portrait or landscape, in the same way that you can shoot your pictures vertically or horizontally. From this box you can click onto 'Properties': this will open yet another box with more options. It will give you a choice of 'Quality Type'. If you are printing a piece of text alongside a photo you can select 'Text and Image'. You can also decide whether you would like to have standard or high quality results with 'Photo' or 'Best Photo'. In order to save ink, use standard quality most of the time.

5 It's also important at this stage to tell the printer what sort of paper or media you will be using. A drop

TROUBLESHOOTING

● If you are having problems printing, use the computer's software to make sure the ink nozzle heads are not clogged and the printing head is clean.

● If the pictures you see on your screen don't look like the pictures you see on your prints, you may have to 'calibrate' your computer and printer. There is easy-to-follow software that will enable you to do this.

● The printer may be rather slow, taking ages to produce an image. Try changing the size of your image and see if that improves things. You may also have too many printing 'jobs' lined up at one time.

down box will enable you to make a selection such as 'Photo Quality Ink Jet Paper', 'Photo Paper' or 'Photo Quality Glossy'. When you have done that, you should check that the correct size of paper is being displayed. Now print away!

Size is: 210 by 297 mm.
A4 | Custom...
Source is:
Auto Select
Type is:
Auto Select

STAND-ALONE PRINTERS

Not many people realise that some printers don't need to be hooked up to a computer. You can link your camera directly to the printer, either via a lead or by placing the digital camera into a docking station.

They are becoming very popular. You can buy 'mobile photo studios': this is a package that will typically consist of a digital camera and a dedicated printer.

These are called 'dye-sublimation' printers. They tend to be smaller than the standard inkjet printer so they are very portable. They operate by heating up dye ribbons to produce a gas. The dye from these ribbons forms the image on the paper. They can produce very high quality results.

There are many different types of paper currently available for photographic prints. They may all look the same, but they vary in price, quality and thickness or weight.

A stand-alone printer with digital camera.

You can buy packs of paper that contain different varieties. Different paper types will produce different results. There's no point in spending time using your skills taking great pictures, only for your paper to let you down.

Multifunction plain paper

This is the relatively cheap, plain white paper that is a very common sight. It's great to use when you are just producing plain text, but it is far from ideal for printing your photographs. This is partly because it doesn't absorb the large amount of ink required for pictures. If you use multifunction paper it will give you very low quality and rather blurred results.

Inkjet paper

This is a popular media type because it is widely available and fairly cheap. It will produce better prints than ordinary paper, but you can't expect top quality results.

Glossy photo paper

Glossy paper has a shiny finish to it, but you can also get high quality, matt, non-shiny paper. This is a good option to go for. It is just like the traditional paper that you can get from a high street photo lab.

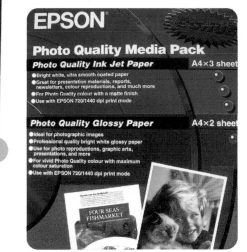

Greeting cards

You can make your own birthday or greeting cards. Using this special type of card will give you good results, and the best thing is that you will have your own pictures on the front of your cards. The packs are available in different colours and in white. If you are using coloured cards, make sure that you do not pick a colour that will clash with the picture you are printing. Remember to adjust the printer so that it can take the slightly thicker sheets of card.

Trendy T-shirts

T-shirts never really go out of fashion but now they are enjoying increased popularity because many top designers are using them to advertise their brand, from Tommy Hilfiger to Ted Baker. Well, now you can create and wear your own work!

You'll need to print your image on to fabric transfer sheets before you can attach it to the T-shirt of your choice. You will also have to select a special paper type on your printer settings.

When you have successfully printed the image, it can be attached to the fabric of the shirt. This is sometimes done by 'ironing' the special sheet of paper directly onto the T-shirt. This process can also be used on certain sweatshirts.

For best results, use images that are saved in TIFF format instead of JPEGs and make sure that your printer is set to at least 150dpi. If you are using an iron to transfer your image onto a T-shirt, make sure you take care not to burn yourself.

Mugs

This is a great gift idea, and it is quite inexpensive to produce. Many photographic shops can do this for you as a special service. One method is to use an industrial heater press. This will press the image onto your desired surface and heat is used to attach the image. They use temperatures of between 375-425 degrees fahrenheit to achieve a permanent fix.

Jigsaws

The first thing to consider when creating your very own personalised puzzle is the actual picture you're hoping to use. If you select a picture with a lot of similarly-coloured areas then you may find it very difficult to complete the puzzle.

This is generally the case with landscape or seascape shots where there can be large areas of similarly-coloured sky. There are companies online as well as high street photo shops that will print your jigsaws for you for a small fee. Sizes vary from 7x5 inches to 16x12 inches.

 A

Aperture

The aperture is the round opening inside the lens. It controls the amount of light that passes through to the image sensor. It is measured in f-stops: f/4, f/5.6, f/8, f/11, f/16, f/22, f/32. The aperture affects the depth of field. As the aperture opens wider, the depth of field decreases.

Archive

This refers to keeping a copy of an image or a file.

Attachment

An attachment can be a document or image file that is sent to someone else in conjunction with an email.

 **B**

Back Up

Making copies of an original image or file on a disc or a hard drive for safekeeping.

Bit

A tiny unit of digital data: eight bits make a single byte.

Blog

This relatively new term refers to a diary that is published on the internet.

Bluetooth

This technology allows wireless communication between specific devices.

 **C**

Calibrate

This is when you adjust a device such as a printer or monitor to a specific setting so that it will produce more accurate results.

Camera Shake

Camera shake reveals itself in the form of blurred or fuzzy images. It occurs particularly in low lighting conditions when the camera is not adequately supported.

DIGITAL PHOTOGRAPHY GLOSSARY

Card Reader
An accessory that accepts the memory card from your camera and can then be linked to your computer to download images.

CCD
CCD stands for 'Charged-Coupled Device'. This is the camera's image sensor.

CD-RW
These are rewritable CDs on which you can record data, and which can be used over and over again.

Cloning
This entails copying one part of an image and placing it in another part of the same scene.

Colour Depth
This refers to the number of colours held within an image. This will have a direct result on the quality of an image.

Colour Saturation
This refers to the strength of the colours contained within a given image.

Compression
When an image is electronically squashed – usually to fit a particular format.

Cropping
Removing part of an image for aesthetic or technical reasons.

Delete
This occurs when an image or file is erased from a memory device on a camera or computer – deliberately or accidentally!

Depth Of Field
The amount of area in front of and behind the main subject that remains in focus. A shallow depth of field will blur the back and foreground whilst a wide depth will allow a larger area to stay in focus.

Digital Zoom
This digital software enlarges a specific area within the image to give the impression of zooming in.

Downloading
The method by which images and data are transferred onto a computer.

Dpi
Dots per square inch: this is how the quality of a printed photograph is measured.

Driver
This is a piece of software required by computers in order to operate peripherals such as printers and scanners.

Exposure
Exposure is the amount of light that passes through the lens and onto the CCD. This is controlled via the shutter and aperture settings.

F-Stop
This denotes the range by which the diaphragm within the lens can be opened and closed at will.

Fill-In

Fill-in is a technique by which light is added into shadowy areas. This can be achieved with a flash, another light source or a special reflector.

Focus

The process by which a lens is adjusted to make a subject sharp.

GIF

Graphic Interchange Format, a popular format predominantly used by website designers.

Gigabyte (Gb)

Consists of one thousand million bytes.

Grayscale

This is a measurement of the increments between black and white.

Hard Copy

An image or document that has been printed out.

Hot-Shoe

An external flashgun can be mounted onto the camera via the hot-shoe connection.

Ink-Jet

The process by which printers spray tiny droplets of ink on paper or another medium to create an image.

Interpolation

This involves increasing the number of pixels in an image in order to improve its overall quality.

Iris

These are the tiny blades housed inside the lens. Their movement alters the size of the aperture.

ISO Speed

This stands for International Standards Organisation and stems from traditional film speed values.

JPEG

Joint Photographic Experts Group: a commonly used format that reduces image files and is useful for easy internet transfer of files.

Kilobyte (Kb)

This equates to 1,024 bytes of information.

LCD

The Liquid Crystal Display is a flat screen used to display information on the back of a camera.

Megabyte (Mb)

Equates to one million bytes.

Megapixel

This is made up of one million pixels.

Memory Card

Removable electronic chip device that is housed in the main body of the camera. It stores the images once they have been captured by the CCD.

Monochrome

Another term for black and white images.

Noise

This is a by-product of using a high speed ISO setting and can make an image appear more grainy.

Optical Zoom
The optical zoom can alter the size of a subject by shifting the lens back and forth.

Overexposure
If too much light passes through the lens onto the CCD it will result in an overexposed or bleached-out image.

Pan
Pivoting a camera smoothly on a horizontal plane to follow an object or create a panoramic effect in the picture.

Palette
A variety of colours or tools available in software programs.

Peripheral
Any device, such as a printer, that is linked to a computer.

Pixel
'Picture Element': the elements or 'building blocks' that make up an image.

RAM
'Random Access Memory': the electronic storage device used by computers.

Reformatting
Preparing a memory card to accept new data.

Resizing
Altering the dimensions or resolution of an image.

Resolution
This is the way in which picture quality is measured. High-resolution images yield good quality results when printed.

Saturation
This relates to the purity of colours.

Sharpening
This is a software tool that gives the impression of greater clarity.

Shutter Lag
This is the delay between pressing the shutter and the camera capturing the image.

TIFF
'Tagged Image File Format': a commonly used file format.

Underexposure
An underexposed image will appear too dark because not enough light has passed through the lens.

Upload
To transfer data from one system to another.

USB
'Universal Serial Bus': a port used to connect cameras to computers and printers.

Virus
A file or program that infiltrates and infects a computer's operating system.

White Balance
This system helps to correct colours when taking images in artificial lighting conditions.

INDEX